ANNE CHISLETT

FLIPPIN' IN

Cornelsen

Anne Chislett
Flippin' In

Herausgegeben von
Albert-Reiner Glaap

Verlagsredaktion
Neil Porter

Technische Umsetzung
Peter Richter

Umschlagfotos
Corel Library

Herausgeber der *Cornelsen Senior English Library*
Prof. Dr. Albert-Reiner Glaap

www.cornelsen.de

1. Auflage, 4. Druck 2007/06

Alle Drucke dieser Auflage sind inhaltlich unverändert
und können im Unterricht nebeneinander verwendet werden.

Druck: CS-Druck CornelsenStürtz, Berlin

ISBN 978-3-464-06821-2

Inhalt gedruckt auf säurefreiem Papier aus nachhaltiger Forstwirtschaft.

CONTENTS

The Characters

Susan	17
Lynn	17
Joe	20–25
Elaine	25–40
Maria	25–50

The Set

Props and set pieces should be consistently stylized to be light-weight and bright. There are lots of props, but a non-realistic minimalism should be kept in mind.

Flippin' In was commissioned and first produced by Young People's Theatre, Toronto, in 1996.

1. McJOBS

A gym, preset with two gear bags.

MARIA, *an immigrant whom we might take for a school cleaner, wheels on the scoreboard. We read Markdale S.S. We read the score of the class teams. Blues: 31. Greens: 28. There should also be a calendar or device that can indicate weeks passing.*

Sound: A referee's whistle; shouts of 'Go!' 'Let's Go! Go, go, go!' from classmates in the stands.

Two sixteen-year-old girls run on. Both wear T-shirts, one with a wildlife concern logo, the other a designer name. SUSAN, *the girl who likes animals, has a green ribbon around her arm to denote her team.* LYNN *has a blue ribbon tied in a neat bow. Both are excited and tense in the last few seconds of the game. They react to invisible other players. Then* SUSAN *seizes the ball and makes a forceful dash for the basket.* LYNN *hesitates for a split second before leaping to block her.* SUSAN *shoots and scores.*

▷ *props:* Requisiten **1** *gym:* Turnhalle · *gear bag:* bag for sports clothes and equipment **3** *scoreboard:* Anzeigetafel · *S.S.* (abbr): Secondary School **5** *device:* Vorrichtung · *indicate sth.:* show sth. **7** *stands* (pl): Zuschauerplatz/-tribüne **9** *logo:* Wortzeichen **10** *ribbon:* Band · *denote sth.:* be a sign of sth. **12** *tense:* angespannt **14** *dash* (n): a sudden run

MARIA *changes the score. Blues: 31. Greens: 30.* SUSAN *regains the ball, ducks around* LYNN, *and sinks what would be the winning basket but –*

Sound: The school bell and the P.E. Instructor's whistle cut short the game. Cheers and boos.

LYNN: That's not fair. Your basket should have counted.

The girls pull off their ribbons and pick up their bags. LYNN*'s is trendier and more expensive than* SUSAN*'s.*

SUSAN: *[shrugging]* There's always next time.

SUSAN *sets off outside with a purpose.* LYNN *seems to need to connect with her.*

LYNN: Susan … wanta come for a coke or something?

SUSAN: *[shaking her head]* I have to go to work.

LYNN: Oh, you're lucky.

SUSAN: See ya.

LYNN: *[refusing the dismissal]* I've been trying to get a job for ages.

And this is surprise enough to make SUSAN *pause.*

SUSAN: You?

LYNN: I've applied at the library, the newspaper, the copy shop …

SUSAN: *[with an edge]* Doesn't your father need another receptionist?

LYNN: You know he's cutting back.

SUSAN: *[knowing this all too well]* Yeah. *[with attitude]* Excuse me.

LYNN: I'm sorry Dad had to lay your mother off, Susan, but it was company policy … you know, orders from head office.

SUSAN: Yeah.

LYNN: Look, it wasn't his fault. *[pause]* And it's not mine either.

JOE *enters and leans on an imaginary corner. He's a rock and rolling tough guy, ring in nose, pins in ears, studs on jacket. He whistles after the girls.* LYNN *glances over.*

SUSAN: Hi, Joe.

LYNN: *[incredulous]* Is he a friend of yours?

SUSAN: *[shrugging]* Sort of. But what do you need to work for?

LYNN: For money of my own. I've a right, don't I?

SUSAN: *[a concession]* I guess.

LYNN: I cannot believe the way you suddenly treat me like I'm a snob or something. *[starting off]* It's just not fair.

SUSAN: *[after her]* Lynn, … well, actually, my boss might be looking for someone.

ELAINE, *an attractive businesswoman in her thirties, enters.*

ELAINE: As long as you have a positive attitude, a friendly personality, and you're willing to work hard, there's a place for you in the Service Industry.

▷ **4** *P.E. Instructor:* Sportlehrer/in **8** *trendy:* fashionable **9** *shrug:* die Achsel zucken **16** *dismissal:* Verabschiedung **20** *with an edge:* scharf, spitz **22** *cut back:* try to spend less money **23** *attitude:* way of behaving (here with coldness, contempt, etc.) **24** *lay sb. off:* dismiss sb. from his or her job **29** *stud:* Niete **32** *incredulous:* unbelieving **35** *concession:* Zugeständnis

MARIA *wheels the scoreboard around to display a billboard of a giant hamburger and a smiling worker.*

ALL: McJobs!

2. KWIK-BITEY WORLD

A fast food franchise

JOE *removes his tough guy accessories until he looks clean cut. Then he and* SUSAN *and* MARIA *pull typical fast food uniforms from* SUSAN*'s bag, and put them on over their clothes as* ELAINE *begins patter #1.* JOE, MARIA, *and* SUSAN *join in as they climb into the uniforms.*

Welcome to KwikWorld
The world of KwikHappy,
Where food is KwikCheap
And service is real snappy.

From Vancouver Island to Bonavista Bay
From Moscow to Paris, from Lima to L.A.
It's bread, meat and potatoes
And 'Have a nice day.'

During the following scene, MARIA *wheels in the needed set pieces and sets up props.*

▷ **1** *display sth.:* show sth. · *billboard:* big board with advertising posters • *franchise:* business which is privately owned but uses the name of a bigger company (e.g. McDonald's, Burger King) **7** *patter:* advertising speech or jingle **12** *snappy:* schwungvoll, flott **17** *wheel sth. in:* etwas hereinfahren

ELAINE: Lynn, tell me why you want to be part of Kwik-Bitey's family?

LYNN: Well... I come here after school and movies and that ... and I think it would be great ... *[smiling]* because it's a great place.

JOE: *[to* SUSAN, *incredulous]* She a friend of yours?

SUSAN: *[shrugging]* Sort of.

ELAINE: You know, you have a lovely smile.

JOE and SUSAN: She's hired.

ALL: We know no regional disparities,
We discount different views
What we sell is similarities
And happy KwikSnappy crews.

On the above line, ELAINE *adds an Employee of the Month poster to the billboard.*

We are bigger than most nations
And a heck of a lot more fun
So take your places at the stations
And be part of Number One

ELAINE: We give you – *[presenting* LYNN *with a uniform from her own bag]* free uniforms!

LYNN: *[dismayed]* Polyester!

JOE: With no pockets.

ELAINE: And a free training video.

LYNN *struggles into her uniform as the others act out the film.* SUSAN *could wear a mask as the actress, and* JOE *a customer's mask. The movements could be somewhat stylised.*

SUSAN: KwikWorld feature presentation! Starring …

JOE: *[donning a mask and bowing]* The happy KwikGuest …

SUSAN: That's customer in English.

ELAINE: It's up to KwikBitey's team to make sure the guest has a positive mental image of our food.

All the dialogue with the exception of ELAINE*'s cheerleading, is rhythmic patter.*

JOE: Our KwikGuest's experience
Begins out of doors.
He sees no litter on the walkways –

ELAINE *drops a candy wrapper and cheerleads as in the basketball game.* MARIA *scurries to pick it up.*

ELAINE: Let's go, gang.

JOE: He'll see sparkling clean floors.

ELAINE: Go, go, go!

MARIA *scurries to wipe the floor.*

From this point on, we take note of the timer.

SUSAN: The On-Counter KwikHostess –

ELAINE: *[reprimanding her]* The nice smiling KwikHostess.
Read the tray liner
Where it says –

▷ **8** *disparity:* difference **9** *discount sth.:* (here) pay no attention to sb./sth. **15** *a heck of a lot:* enorm viel mehr **20** *dismayed:* shocked, unpleasantly surprised **37** *scurry:* run quickly with short steps **38** *gang:* Leute **42** *timer:* Zeitmesser, Stoppuhr **44** *reprimand sb.:* tell sb. off **45** *tray liner:* (in a fast food restaurant) paper that covers a tray

LYNN: *[searching]* Oh ... *[reading]* oh –
Smiles are free!

SUSAN: *[donning a smiling mask]*
Welcome to our restaurant.
May I take your order, please?

JOE: *[hamming it up]*
I'll have a chocolate shake
And the big one with cheese.

SUSAN: A whopping big KwikKing, sir?

JOE: Yeah, that should suffice.

ELAINE: *[prompting]* And?

SUSAN: And will you have some fries, sir?

JOE: Yeah, fries might be kinda nice.

ELAINE: *[to* LYNN*]*
The profit-making order
Includes French fries and a drink.
If KwikGuest omits an item
We need to make him think.

LYNN: Oh.

SUSAN: *[entering the order on the cash register]*
Two dollars, fifty cents, sir.
Now, is that to go or stay?
Depending on his answer,
Grab a bag or grab a tray.

ELAINE: Cut to!

JOE *takes off his mask and runs or jumps to the area we establish as the kitchen.* MARIA *takes a place along the grill*

JOE: Meanwhile, back in the KwikKitchen, the computerised Kwik cash register has relayed the order to the cooking crew. In English, that's 'grill toads.'

ELAINE: Fries.

JOE *and* MARIA *have a mime/dance/patter number which establishes the symbolic props and kitchen layout. The kitchen has a different rhythm.*

MARIA: *[speaking with an accent]* Thank you.

JOE:
They came out of the freezer this morning,
They're in baskets all ready to go
Pre-cut, measured, and coated with sugar
To give them that yummy brown glow.

JOE *lowers a basket and pushes a button.*

ELAINE: Cheeseburger.

MARIA *places a burger and the grill.*

JOE:
So you put down the heel
And slap on the cheese
Then dab on the mustard,
Give ketchup a squeeze. *[squeezing twice]*

ELAINE: *[correcting him]* One squeeze, and in a spiral motion starting from the outside edge.

▷ **3** *don sth.:* to put sth. (e.g. clothes) on **6** *ham it up:* act in a humorous, exaggerated way **10** *suffice:* be enough **11** *prompt sb.:* help sb. by suggesting sth. **17** *omit sth.:* leave sth. out **24** *grab sth.:* take sth. quickly **25** *cut to!:* (here) change from one area to another **26** *establish sth. as sth. else:* come to realize that sth. is sth. else **29** *relay sth.:* to pass sth. on **30** *toad:* Kröte **38** *measure sth.:* check the length of sth. **39** *yummy:* tasty, delicious **43** *heel:* Absatz, vorspringendes Teil, Hebel **45** *mustard:* Senf

JOE: Then you pick up the pickle
And spoon on the onion …

ELAINE: Hold the pickle! Joe, can't you even get it right in the video?

SUSAN: The onion goes on first.

ELAINE: Rewind.

In fast backward motion JOE *takes off the pickle and scoops up the onion.*

Play.

JOE *puts on the onion, then the pickle.*

People can taste the difference.

Sound: Buzzers and beeps.

JOE: That sound tells you the fries are ready
This one signals the burger is done
You put it together in its own special wrapper …

LYNN: *[continuing his rhythm]*
It looks so easy!
It looks like fun!

ELAINE: We've taken the worry from working
We've laid out what you say and you do
You must follow Kwik-Biteys' fool-proof system
It's all tried and tested and true.

JOE: A dog with hands could do this job.

ELAINE: I beg your pardon?

JOE: Nothing.

ELAINE: No, I want to know what you said!

SUSAN: *[quickly]* Hey ... here comes the burger.

MARIA: *[presenting the burger to* SUSAN*]* Straights up!

SUSAN: Mr. KwikGuest?

JOE *puts on his mask.*

Have a nice day.

ELAINE: Stop the clock. Two minutes, forty seconds.

ELAINE *takes the burger from* JOE *and gives it to* LYNN.

LYNN: Wow. Thanks.

JOE: *[sotto to* SUSAN*]* What a dork.

ELAINE: So, how does it compare with burgers you've eaten elsewhere?

LYNN: Burgers are burgers, I guess.

ELAINE: Right, Lynn, that's why we don't sell taste. Gang, tell her what we sell?

JOE and SUSAN: S.O.S.

ELAINE: *[to* LYNN*]* Do you know what S.O.S. stands for?

LYNN: Like 'Help'? If you're out in a boat or something ... 'Save our Souls'?

▷ **1** *pickle:* pickled (= eingelegt) vegetable; (here) gherkin **11** *buzzer:* Summer **14** *wrapper:* Verpackung **20** *fool-proof:* narrensicher **23** *I beg your pardon?:* Wie bitte? **34** *sotto:* quietly · *dork* (sl): fool

JOE, SUSAN and MARIA: Speed of Service!
[in rhythm]

If you're a mother who's too tired
Or a traveller running late
The food may not be gourmet
But you never have to wait.

Sound: Cars, doors opening, footsteps, conversation. A crowd of customers.

SUSAN: *[warning]* The movie's out!

ELAINE: Pre-cook twelve straights please.

JOE: Thank you.

Sound: A montage of recorded orders, whirring of exhaust fans, sizzling beef, shake makers, bells, whistles and buzzes from other devices.

ELAINE: Let's go, gang!

SUSAN: *[to customer]* Have a nice day. *[to kitchen]* Three fries.

JOE *is flipping and* MARIA *is assembling burgers, double time from the event before. She shoves the burgers to* SUSAN *who bags them and gives them to the imaginary customers.*

JOE: Thank you.

SUSAN: Have nice day. *[to kitchen]* Big one, no cheese.

ELAINE: Lynn, put on your hat!

JOE: Thank you.

SUSAN: May I take your order, please.

ELAINE: Now, go, go, go!

LYNN *hesitates, then dives in and aces the smile.*

LYNN: *[sticking the hat on]* And will you have fries with that?

SUSAN: Have a nice day.

Sound: Sting. The rush is over. Everyone slumps relaxed.

ELAINE: *[rousing herself, to* SUSAN, JOE *and* MARIA*]* Don't stop. If there's time to lean, there's time to clean. *[she sets an example by wiping a surface as she speaks to* LYNN*]* Kid, you're going to have your picture up there *[pointing to the billboard]* in no time.

JOE: I've never been employee of the month.

MARIA: May I go to bathroom now?

ELAINE: Well, if you have to, but don't be long. *[continuing to* LYNN, *as* MARIA *scurries off]* Lynn, you can take over the counter. *[turning to* SUSAN*]* Susan, I'm moving you to dining room hostess.

SUSAN: *[protesting]* Elaine ...

ELAINE: I'm sorry, you just won't smile enough. *[she exits]*

LYNN: Dining room hostess ... that sounds great.

SUSAN *takes or mimes a cloth and mop and begins cleaning.*

JOE: In English that's floor washer and toilet scrubber.

LYNN: Oh ...

SUSAN: Don't worry about it.

▷ **10** *straight:* Schnellgericht **12** *whir:* schwirren, surren · *exhaust fan:* ventilator which removes the smell of cooking **13** *sizzling:* zischend **17** *double time:* twice as fast **18** *shove sth.:* push sth. **26** *ace sth.:* do sth. very well **29** *sting:* (here) high-pitched sound **30** *rouse yourself:* become active **31** *lean:* anlehnen, sich ausruhen **32** *surface:* Arbeitsfläche **40** *exit:* leave the stage

LYNN: I'll tell her I won't do it. I mean it, Susan.

MARIA *runs back on.*

SUSAN: *[shrugging]* She'd only find someone else.

LYNN: It's totally not fair if I take your job.

SUSAN: Lynn, you're replacing a guy who worked here three years … until he talked back to Elaine.

LYNN: But she seems … kinda nice.

MARIA: Before. *[looking at her]* Before she was nice. Not now.

JOE: Not since they sent her to Burger U.

LYNN: What's that?

JOE: Kwik-Bitey's has these courses for managers. Elaine just got promoted.

SUSAN: *[to the point]* Look, whatever job I'm doing, the money's the same. And in six months I can apply for a KwikScholarship.

LYNN: They'll give you a scholarship?

SUSAN: If Elaine recommends me. I can't afford to make waves.

Sound: Bridge.

JOE: Red crew's here.

JOE *and* MARIA *put the leftover burgers in a bag.*

LYNN: You don't throw those away, do you?

JOE: We have to leave them for the boss to count.

SUSAN: She throws them away.

LYNN: Shouldn't they be given to the homeless, or something?

SUSAN: *[exasperated]* Lynn …

MARIA: Smiles are free.

SUSAN: But only smiles.

MARIA *puts containers etc. in a garbage bag.*

LYNN: We could at least recycle the paper.

SUSAN: *[really exasperated]* Lynn! Chill!

JOE: *[in unison with Susan]* Chill!

JOE *starts putting rings and pins back on.*

LYNN: So … Susan, I have the car if you want a ride.

SUSAN: *[shaking her head]* I'm meeting someone.

LYNN: Someone … like Jerry?

JOE: Jerry, eh? Who's Jerry?

SUSAN: Bug off!

LYNN: *[to* MARIA*]* How about you? Would you like a drive home?

MARIA: *[to* LYNN*]* Yes, please. Thank you.

▷ **6** *talk back to sb.*: jdm. widersprechen **11–12** *get promoted:* be given a better job in a company **16** *make waves* (infml): cause trouble **17** *bridge:* sound that indicates some sort of change is taking place **24** *exasperated:* erbost, genervt **29** *chill:* relax **36** *bug off:* lass mich in Ruhe

JOE: I could use a lift. *[*LYNN *hesitates]* I wouldn't ask but my mom's waiting to unload my kid.

LYNN: *[indredulous]* You have a kid?

JOE: *[defensively]* What's the matter with that?

LYNN: Nothing ... it's just I didn't think of you being married, that's all.

SUSAN: *[warning]* Lynn.

JOE: Who said I was married?

LYNN: Oh. Well, sure I can drive you.

JOE *turns away to pick up his gear.*

MARIA: *[to* LYNN*]* His woman – run away.

LYNN: She left her baby?

SUSAN: Shh.

LYNN: With him?

JOE: Ready?

ELAINE: *[entering]* Gang, we're short of a crew member. Would you stay on, please ... Joe?

JOE: Gee, Elaine ...

ELAINE: Last week you were begging for extra hours.

JOE: Yeah, like if I know a bit in advance, eh?

ELAINE: *[turning to* SUSAN*]* Susan?

SUSAN: *[pause]* Elaine, really, any other night I'd be glad to ...

LYNN: *[jumping in]* I can stay.

ELAINE: You're not trained on grill yet. *[turning to* MARIA*]* Maria, I'm sure I can count on you?

MARIA: *[by rote]* Yes, Elaine. Thank you.

ELAINE *exits.*

LYNN: *[after her]* Elaine ... *[but she's gone, to* SUSAN*]* I forgot to ask what the pay was.

SUSAN: Take a guess.

ALL: Everyone's disposable
That's the order of the day
When unemployment is at maximum
You're content with minimum pay.

SUSAN: There are kids who save for college

LYNN: Or to buy the latest rage.

ALL: There's a line up at the counter
For jobs at minimum wage.

JOE: There are men who worked in factories
Till their jobs migrated south.

MARIA: There's an army of weary women
Who are living hand to mouth.

▷ **2** *unload sb.:* hand sb. over **9** *gear:* stuff **25** *by rote:* (here) say sth. in an automatic way **29** *take a guess:* rate mal **30** *disposable:* sth. that can be discarded or thrown away when it is no longer needed or when it no longer works **33** *minimum pay:* Mindestlohn **39** *migrate:* move **40** *weary:* tired

ALL: KwikJobs are dull and boring,
but you're in out of the rain,
though every job leads nowhere,
and every job's the same.

Minding machines month by month
Will make your brain go numb,
While you're putting in time at minimum pay
And waiting for a break to come.

The actors set up the crew room. This could mean simply striking props off the counter. They might add seats. JOE *and* SUSAN *exit.*

LYNN and MARIA:
Hoping that a break will come.
Praying that a break will come.

The date on the board is changed to three months later as the song segues to commercial tone. In the crew room.

3. Grievances

JOE *enters and places a cut-out ghetto blaster, on loud. His shirt is unbuttoned. Sound: Some raucous hit-parade tape.*

SUSAN: *[entering, her hat still in her hand, she changes the date to January]* Maria not here? *[He can't hear her, she turns the ghetto blaster down]* Have you seen Maria?

JOE: They called her in early ... to replace Bob Sung on green crew.

SUSAN: Bob sick?

JOE: Nope. *[*SUSAN *looks at him]* Elaine ran out of milk last night. *[buttoning his shirt]* Guess who she found behind the counter at the 7–11?

SUSAN: *[pause]* Bummer.

JOE: What law says you can't hold down two jobs, eh?

SUSAN: Joe, you got something on your shirt.

▷ **6** *numb:* not being able to feel sth. **9** *strike sth. off:* (here) take sth. off **15** *segue:* change slowly from one sound to another • *grievance:* complaint **16** *ghetto blaster* (sl): large radio **17** *raucous* ['rɔːkəs]: loud and rough **25** *7-11:* general store that stays open from 7am till 11 pm **26** *bummer:* Pech gehabt

JOE: I didn't make the laundromat.

SUSAN: Better ask Elaine to rent you one.

JOE: *[explaining his plan]* I get to the grill before she sees me … I say I spilled some grease … like just now.

SUSAN: She's still going make you change.

JOE: She lends me a shirt … free.

SUSAN: In your dreams.

JOE: She's conned two bucks out of me so far this week

SUSAN: I know, but –

JOE: I lost my name tag. Seventy-five cents. She fined me for smoking in the parking lot. That cap for the softball game against Wendy's …

LYNN *enters in time to hear softball game.*

LYNN: That was fun. *[they look at her]* Well, I scored three hits.

JOE: I had to pay a whole dollar for the cap!

LYNN: Yeah … But the money's for a good cause.

JOE: What about my cause? 'Cause I earn my money and I want to take it home.

SUSAN: Going up there in a dirty uniform is asking for a bad scene.

LYNN: Where's Maria?

SUSAN *points upwards.*

JOE: What's all this about Maria?

LYNN: We're supposed to meet her ... a half-hour before our shift.

SUSAN: *[to* LYNN*]* Hey, you didn't tell us – how did your three month evaluation go?

LYNN: Elaine heard me offer some customer a packet of ketchup.

JOE: *[laughing]* There goes your shot at employee of the month.

SUSAN: *[mimicking the Boss]* You must learn to think globally. If every hostess in every Kwik-Bitey's gave away more condiments than she was asked for ...

JOE: Our profits would drop to only seven-hundred billion zillion a year.

MARIA *enters.* SUSAN *goes to switch radio stations.*

LYNN: Hi, Maria.

MARIA: Sorry, sorry.

RADIO HOST: ... our caller from Brampton, and what's on your mind?

MARIA: *[imitating what's she's just heard on the radio]* And what on your mind?

LYNN: *[to* MARIA*]* 'What's'. That is short for 'what is'.

JOE: *[turning the radio off]* Get a life.

MARIA *points to* LYNN *and* SUSAN *by way of explanation.*

MARIA: I learn – I am learning English.

▷ **1** *make sth.:* (here) get to sth. · *laundromat:* Waschsalon **4** *grease:* Fett **8** *con sth. out of sb.:* cheat sb. to get sth. **11** *cap:* Käppi **23** *shift:* Arbeitsschicht **25** *evaluation:* Beurteilung, Auswertung **27** *there goes your shot at sth.* (infml): that's the end of your attempt to be sth. **28** *mimic sb.:* jdn. nachmachen **29** *condiments:* things that are added to food to give flavour

LYNN: Joe, we're helping Maria practice.

SUSAN: *[to* Joe*]* You get outta bed on the wrong side this morning?

JOE: I'm tired, that's all.

SUSAN: The baby still waking you up?

JOE: She's got a tooth coming ...

MARIA: Tooth?

SUSAN: *[pointing to one of hers]* Tooth. Baby tooth.

MARIA: Oh ... *[understanding, to* JOE*]* She cry all night.

LYNN: I remember baby-sitting my niece –

JOE: *[over her]* I thought it was a fever, so I took her to emerge. The nurses looked at me like I was a Klingon. How was I supposed to know, eh?

SUSAN: Why didn't you call your mother?

JOE: 'Cause I'm calling her all the time. And she's got problems of her own. *[pause]* Cause she thinks I'm crazy. The nurses think I'm crazy. Maybe I am crazy.

SUSAN: I don't think you're crazy.

JOE: But if I give her up ... Mom was telling me you can choose now ... I could pick her out a doctor or a lawyer ... or one of those rich computer types.

SUSAN: A nerd? *[*JOE *shrugs]* I'd hate having a nerd for my father.

JOE: Even a rich one?

SUSAN: Oh, yeah. I bet she'd hate it too.

JOE: Maybe. Yeah. *[cheering up]* She'd hate it.

ELAINE *enters with a typed schedule which she can tape on the billboard.*

Oh, Elaine, I need to rent a shirt.

ELAINE: In a minute. *[to everyone]* Gang, we're falling below company standard on fry yield. There'll be a bonus for the first shift that hits the target.

She starts off. MARIA *takes a quick glance at the schedule.*

MARIA: *[coming forward]* Elaine … me … I … on grill all the time?

SUSAN: You promised her some time on the counter.

JOE *goes to the schedule.*

ELAINE: *[as in 'get real']* Susan …

LYNN: Her comprehension's great. She's just shy about speaking …

SUSAN: Maria, show her.

MARIA: *[virtually accentless]* Welcome to our restaurant. May I take your order please?

ELAINE: That's quite an improvement, Maria.

MARIA: Will you have fries with that?

ELAINE: Unfortunately, the problem isn't your accent … *[carefully]* It's company policy … Our guests expect a certain image.

▷ **2** *get outta (= out of) bed the wrong side:* be in a bad temper **10** *emerge = emergency:* Notfallstation **11** *Klingon:* alien life form in the TV series *Star Trek* **21** *nerd* (infml): boring person who is interested in computers **29** *fry yield:* (here) the amount of food sold **38** *virtually:* almost

SUSAN: Like 'cute'?

ELAINE: Like happy. Fun. Young

JOE: *[reacting to the schedule]* What the hell …

ELAINE: Watch your language, please.

JOE: You marked me down for three-and-a-half hours.

SUSAN *rushes to look at the schedule, followed by* MARIA.

I'm not a part timer, eh? I do a minimum of six.

SUSAN: We've only got seventeen hours for the whole week. I mean … that's all anybody has … total!

MARIA: Mistake, yes? Mistake?

ELAINE: I'm sorry, Maria. *[to everybody]* Kwik-Bitey's has decided that the staff must look fresh all the time. We can't have tired, irritable employees around our guests.

JOE: When was I irritable? Tell me when?

LYNN: *[warning]* Joe …

MARIA: *[with a touch of panic]* I never tired. Never.

ELAINE: Maria, it's nothing personal. We need you to be on your toes … to look like you're having fun.

JOE: Hey Maria … I'm on my toes. *[twirling her around]*
We're KwikHappy
We're KwikSnappy, –

ELAINE: You're insubordinate!

Silence.

JOE: Elaine, look ... please ... Five days of three-and-a-half hours. That's around a hundred bucks.

ELAINE: You'll still get discounts on food.

JOE *bangs the table and turns away.*

Joe, I won't put up with this.

JOE: I been working here for two lousy years.

LYNN: *[cautiously]* It doesn't seem very fair. I mean it's okay for Susan and me, but –

SUSAN: Not for me. My mother's lost her job, remember.

JOE: I can't make it on a hundred ... there's no way.

ELAINE: It's a new directive from the head office. I'm sorry, but there's nothing I can do. Now, *[glancing at the clock or her watch]* you're on deck in five. Oh ... Maria, you've already done four hours. I have to send you home. *[she exits]*

LYNN: I cannot believe this. It's so ... simply unfair.

JOE: I'd do better on pogey.

SUSAN: You won't get unemployment if you quit. Not for ages anyway.

LYNN: *[full of sympathy for* JOE*]* It's absolutely not fair.

JOE: *[taking out his anger on her]* Will you stop saying that!

LYNN: Well, it isn't. And somebody should do something!

▷ **5** *mark sb. down:* put sb. on a list or schedule **14** *irritable:* easily annoyed and made angry **19** *twirl sb. around:* jdn. herumwirbeln **22** *insubordinate:* rude, disobedient **25** *buck:* dollar **29** *lousy* (infml): miserable **36** *be on deck in five:* be working in five minutes **39** *on pogey* (Canadian English): unemployment money

JOE: Yeah, missy prissy? Like who?

SUSAN: Don't call her that.

JOE: Okay, you tell me who's going to do something?

SUSAN: I don't know …

JOE: Nobody! 'Cause Elaine says 'it's my way or the highway'. And there's nothing anybody can do. Absolutely sweet stinking nothing. *[he exits]*

LYNN: *[to Maria]* Don't worry, Maria … it'll be all right.

LYNN *exits.* SUSAN *stands, looking at* MARIA. *She touches her shoulder before exiting.* MARIA *exits.*

4. Taking Action

LYNN *is walking home.* SUSAN *runs after her. Both are out of uniform.*

SUSAN: Lynn ... wait up?

LYNN: I thought you'd be meeting Jerry.

SUSAN: He's studying for French. Where's your car?

LYNN: Home. I'm walking off the fat I eat here.

SUSAN: Listen, I was thinking about Joe and Maria ... and about Bob Sung too.

LYNN: The guy who got fired?

SUSAN: Yeah. Like Joe said, there's no law against having two part-time jobs.

LYNN: No law at all.

SUSAN: And ... well ... I was thinking about my mother ... *[*LYNN *winces]* Your dad had to pay her a severance, right?

▷ **1** *missy prissy* (infml): name for a person who acts in a prim or prudish way **24** *wince:* zusammenzucken · *severance:* payment by a firm to employees who lose their jobs because of cutbacks in the workforce

LYNN: He manages the place. He doesn't own it.

SUSAN: Yeah, but he couldn't just say … 'You're out of here,' like Elaine did to Bob.

LYNN: Dad's not a mean person. Honestly, Susan, he's not.

SUSAN: Okay, okay. But when the rumours started … that there were going to be lay offs … I remember mom saying, 'At least we have a union. We'll have a bit of protection.'

LYNN: *[uncomfortably]* Actually, I don't think dad agrees with unions much.

SUSAN: But maybe you could ask him … like what he was allowed to do, and what he wasn't?

LYNN: Why don't you ask your mother?

SUSAN: She told me to keep my mind on my scholarship.

LYNN: What's the point anyway? I mean, we don't have a union.

SUSAN: Yeah … Except … they started one at Harvey's.

LYNN: Harvey's?

SUSAN: As in McDonald's, Wendy's, KFC, Burger King, Kwik-Bitey's? This guy at Harvey's started a union. It was in the paper last winter.

LYNN: Susan … don't even think about it.

SUSAN: Why? You said it yourself. Somebody has to do something.

LYNN: I didn't mean us.

SUSAN: *[shrugging]* Who else is there?

LYNN: The full-time people.

SUSAN: Except there aren't any after today, remember?

LYNN: Okay, I mean adults.

SUSAN: Most of the adults who work here are like Joe or Maria. They're kinda at a disadvantage.

LYNN: Okay ... but ... was the guy who started the union at Harvey's still in high school?

SUSAN: I don't remember. But maybe I should make like it's a school project and hit the library.

SUSAN *and* LYNN *exit.*

▷ **6** *lay offs:* job losses **17** *as in ...* (infml): (here) it's like ... · *KFC:* Kentucky Fried Chicken **32** *hit sth.* (sl): go to sth.

5. Reaction

From a different direction JOE *and* MARIA *enter the break room.* MARIA *changes the date on the board to a week later.*

JOE: *[imitating Nicholson's Hoffa]* 'Put down that bleep bleep burger, you bleep bleeper!' You see that movie?

MARIA: *[reacting in fear]* I don't want fight … I don't want strike.

LYNN *enters, buttoning her uniform top.*

LYNN: I guess Susan's been talking to you about her idea?

JOE: She's been talking to everybody, eh? All week.

LYNN: So, like – what do people on the other shifts think?

SUSAN *enters in uniform.*

JOE: Oh, you know …
Unions are run by the mafia.
If you judge by Hollywood.
They're full of low riff-raff –

MARIA: Eee-ah.

JOE: Who needs a bunch of hoods?

SUSAN: Did you guys ever see *Norma Rae*, or *Silkwood* or *Matewan*? *[they all shake their heads]* Well, rent a movie and check out the other side of the story.

LYNN: I guess there's good and bad people in unions, just like there is in management.

SUSAN: Way back in a bygone age
Working days were twelve hours long
Even children slaved for starvation wages
And no one called it wrong.
But workers struggled to unite
Or it still would be that way
Unions fought for every right
Most folks enjoy today.

JOE: Hey, that's crappola.

SUSAN: No, I looked it up ... Unions won the right to have pensions, and sick benefits, and safe working conditions ... Or compensation if you do get hurt on the job. Like the right to have a vacation with pay. Like the right to be treated as if you counted for something instead of like you were dirt.

LYNN: That sounds like propaganda to me.

SUSAN: I'm not asking you to take my word. I'm asking you to check it out for yourself.

LYNN: But even if what you're saying is true ... like dad says 'That was then. This is now.'
Ancient history's a sedative
This is the nineties, eh?
You have to be competitive.

▷ **3** *Hoffa:* film about corrupt union boss Jimmy Hoffa starring Jack Nicholson **14** *riff-raff:* Gesindel **17–18** *Norma Rae, Silkwood, Matewan:* films in which companies treat their employees badly **22** *bygone age:* a long time ago **30** *crappola* (sl): rubbish **41** *sedative:* drug that makes you sleepy or relaxed

SUSAN: Or so experts always say.

LYNN: Put collective bargains on the shelf.

JOE: Who wants to share slim pickin's?
It's every man for himself –

LYNN: Or herself …

SUSAN: As the elephant tells the chickens.

LYNN: What you have to understand is that we are in a post-industrial economy.

SUSAN: Yeah, but what does that mean?

LYNN: It means anyone who's got a job, even a temporary job, is really lucky.

SUSAN: Look, guys – I don't understand much about economics and all that – but it makes sense to me that – well – as long as it's a great big company against Joe, or Maria or you or me … well … none of us has a chance, right? But if we had an organisation that could go to bat for us … well … we might have a chance – that's all.

JOE: Chill!

ELAINE *enters with an 'audit type' form.*

ELAINE: Did anyone eat any burgers without writing it down?

MARIA *shakes her head nervously.*

JOE: Not me.

ELAINE: Who put the waste in the bag?

JOE: I did …

ELAINE: How many patties?

JOE: I don't remember ... four or five, maybe.

ELAINE: There was one when I looked this morning.

JOE: *[looking at the floor]* Like I said, I don't remember.

MARIA *shakes her head.*

ELAINE: There's nearly a pound-and-a-half of meat unaccounted for. Joe, you know stealing food is instant dismissal?

JOE: Elaine, I swear ... I didn't take so much as a chip.

ELAINE: This better not happen again. *[she stares at him for a long beat]* Or you're outta here. *[pause]* Lynn, you were short on cash ... two dollars and forty cents.

LYNN: This guy ordered, and then –

ELAINE: *[cutting her off]* The money will be deducted from your next cheque.

ELAINE *exits.*

JOE: Bitch. *[to* SUSAN*]* So, about this union ... how do I sign up?

SUSAN: We have to find one to join first.

LYNN: Hey, guys, slow down –

JOE: *[to* SUSAN*]* You find one.

▷ **2** *bargains:* Verhandlungen, Abkommen **3** *slim pickin's:* small reward for your labour **16** *bat for sb.:* auf der Seite von jemandem kämpfen **18** *audit type form:* form on which everything which is used must be written down **24** *patty:* (here) burger **29** *unaccounted for:* missing **30** *instant dismissal*: sofortige Entlassung **36** *deduct sth.:* take sth. off **39** *bitch* (sl): Sau

SUSAN: No, this is something we should all do together.

LYNN: Look, I admit Elaine is being unfair –

JOE: *[cutting her off, to* SUSAN*]* You're the one who knows about this stuff. You get it going, I'll sign up.

SUSAN: *[hesitating]* Okay. *[exiting]* I'll get back to you.

JOE *follows her off.*

MARIA: *[calling after her]* No, Susan, please, no.

LYNN: Maria, nobody has to get involved if they don't want to, you know.

MARIA: You are nice girl, Lynn. But you understand nothing.

MARIA *exits.* LYNN *stands a moment, then follows her.*

Sound: Bridge.

SUSAN'S *home. The date is changed to the next day.*

SUSAN *enters, out of uniform, with a portable phone tucked under her ear, a list of numbers in one hand and a pencil or pen in the other.*

SUSAN: *[into the phone]* Me? I'm seventeen. *[pause]* But what difference ... *[pause]* Oh. Does that go for all unions?

LYNN enters, out of uniform.

SUSAN: *[pause]* Okay. *[automatically]* Have a nice day.

LYNN: Your mother let me in.

SUSAN: Yeah?

LYNN: Dad had this party and there was all these leftovers ... so I suggested I'd drive it all to the Food Bank ...

SUSAN: So ...

▷ **14** *tucked:* festgeklemmt **24** *food bank:* place where poor people go to get free food

LYNN: Maria was there ... with her four little kids. They were picking up stuff. So – I guess if you're willing to risk your scholarship ...

SUSAN: I don't want to, but I can't let Kwik-Bitey's treat Joe and Maria this badly.

LYNN: I can't either. I just hope dad never finds out.

SUSAN: *[giving her the slip of paper]* Call out the numbers. I'm at the fifth one down.

LYNN: 747-6051.

SUSAN *punches in the phone number.*

SUSAN: *[into the phone]* Hi, I want to speak to a union organiser.

LYNN: So all the crossed out ones said no?

SUSAN: Yeah. *[into the phone]* Fast Food. *[pause]* Part time. ... Yeah, grade 12 ... Seventeen, but listen ... *[pause]* Right. Have a nice day. *[to* LYNN*]* Next?

LYNN: 1-800-265-2189. You know, I wish you'd stop saying 'Have a nice day.'

SUSAN: I didn't, did I?

LYNN: You do all the time. Even in school.

SUSAN: You're kidding – *[into the phone]* Hi, hello. May I speak with an organiser, please? *[to* LYNN*]* Do I really?

LYNN: I did it to Mr. Wachuk after English. He said 'Sorry, I've made other plans.'

SUSAN: Jerry says he can't tell if I'm smiling because of him, or ... *[into the phone]* Oh, yes. I'm looking for information on how to join your union. *[pause]* Why do you ask that? *[pause]* Oh, I have a young voice, that's all. Actually, I'm quite old really.

LYNN: Susan!

SUSAN: A committee? *[she gives the high sign to* LYNN*]* Yes, as a matter of fact we have – just now – formed a committee. *[pause]* On all shifts? ... ah ... about sixty-two. But that would include the boss and *[pause]* ... not the managers?

LYNN: Minus Elaine and ... three assistants. Fifty-eight.

SUSAN: The committee secretary says we have fifty-eight workers. *[pause]* Mine? What for? *[pause]* Oh, Oh, great! 2910 Markdale Drive. M9Z 4Y2. Thanks. Have a – I mean, goodbye.

LYNN: What's happening?

SUSAN: He's sending us a guidelines package!

LYNN: Then ... we'll have a union?

SUSAN: All we have to do is sign up fifty-five percent of all the guys who work at the franchise ... Fifty-five percent of fifty-eight?

LYNN: *[reaching into her purse]* The secretary requires her calculator.

SUSAN: We're going to need everybody's phone number. You'll have to get the master list and photocopy it.

LYNN: *[looking up from her calculator]* Me?

▷ **9** *punch sth.* (e.g. *a button*): press sth. **28** *give the high sign:* raise one's hand with the palm and fingers stretched out **42** *calculator:* Taschenrechner

SUSAN: Say you want to send out party invitations or something. *[seeing* LYNN*'s face]* Elaine likes you ... She won't suspect anything.

LYNN: Can't we just ask for a list?

SUSAN: Listen, if the boss finds out about this, we're hamburger.

Sound: The phone rings. They both jump.

LYNN: It's not possible.

SUSAN: *[nervous]* Hello ... *[relieved]* Oh, Jerry, I'll call you back, okay? *[pause]* Because I'm real busy. [*short pause*] I'll tell you about it later. Gotta go. *[hanging up, to* LYNN*]* So, what's the magic number?

LYNN: Thirty-one point nine.

SUSAN: Point nine? I guess that's Joe! *[they laugh]* Hey, hey, Lynn ... we can do this thing! *[they run off]*

Sound: Musical Bridge

7. Signing up

Music under a choreographed, stylised section as Joe *turns the billboard to reveal the scoreboard. The teams are now designated 'Yes' and 'No'.* Elaine *changes the date.* Maria *passes out hand-held masks which they hold before their faces and create personalities – like real fast – as* Lynn *and* Susan *enter and dash about persuading people to sign cards.*

Susan: *[offering a card]* Sign for dignity, respect …

Mask: Can we take a leak without asking? *[YES: 1]*

Cool Mask: A union is something … I might picture myself joining … if I were like … dead. *[NO: 1]*

During the rest of the dialogue the scoreboard is changed by the actors with the NO side taking the lead.

Lynn: Sign for more fair treatment.

Mask: How about better wages?

Lynn: *[uncertain]* For sure.

Susan: Well … we can negotiate a contract … *[YES: 7]*

▷ **18** *pass sth. out:* etwas verteilen **31** *negotiate sth.:* etwas verhandeln

MASK: Sounds great.

LYNN: *[to another]* They won't be able to fire you.

SUSAN: Not without just cause.

MASK: I guess I'm just not a labour sort of person.

LYNN: You work here.

MASK: It's only temporary. *[NO: 11]*

SUSAN: *[to another]* Sure, there are dues, *[NO: 13]* but not very much when you consider. *[YES: 10]*

COOLEST MASK: Not. *[NO: 16]*

LYNN: Why not?

COOLER MASK: Because *[gesturing elegantly]* I live in the world.

SUSAN: *[to another]* Seniority will count.

The YES side of the scoreboard starts to catch up.

LYNN: *[to another]* You've heard of empowerment, haven't you?

MASK: The bosses aren't going to give us anything unless we show strength. *[YES: 14]*

SUSAN: *[to another]* Sign here and we'll have input into scheduling.

The numbers on the YES side mount quickly.

MASK: Things couldn't get worse. *[YES: 21]*

MASK: My old man was a miner. He says the union saved his life.

MASK: It's good you're doing this. Thank you. *[YES: 33]*

CHORUS: Thank you, Susan. We're with you all the way.

The scoreboard flips to: YES: 42. NO: 16.

SUSAN: Forty-two out of fifty-eight!

LYNN: That's more than fifty-five percent.

SUSAN: *[jumping up and down]* We did it!

Sound: Cheers.

JOE: We have our union?

SUSAN: We send in the cards, the labour board certifies us, then we have our union!

LYNN: It's a piece of cake!

SUSAN: It's a big one with cheese!

LYNN: Watch out, Kwik-Bitey's!

SUSAN: We're going to make things better for everybody.

LYNN: After the shift … let's go celebrate.

JOE: I'm broke.

SUSAN: You'll have more money soon.

LYNN: My treat for now.

JOE: Yea, Susan … Yea, Lynn.

▷ **7** *dues:* money to be paid **14** *empowerment:* act of assuming power for yourself **17** *input:* (here) the right to have your say about sth. · *schedule sth.:* (here) plan sth. (e.g. shifts) **31** *a piece of cake* (infml): easy **36** *be broke:* have no money left **38** *my treat:* ich lade dich ein

All sing a high-spirited rendition of one verse of 'Solidarity Forever', during which the break room props are removed and the restaurant restored. The date is changed to three days later. June. LYNN *and* SUSAN *don full uniform. Before the last few words,* ELAINE *enters. Big Silence.* LYNN, JOE, SUSAN *and* MARIA *take their places for work.*

8. Discovery

LYNN: Welcome to our restaurant. May I take your order, please?

Sound: Taped orders, and the noises of the machines at a fairly slow pace.

ELAINE: Susan, you're on the counter. Lynn …

She beckons to LYNN. LYNN *and* SUSAN *exchange a glance as* LYNN *follows* ELAINE *to a corner.*

Lynn, you're one of the best workers I ever had here …

LYNN: Oh, I … thanks.

ELAINE: You're intelligent, enthusiastic … and you're popular.

LYNN: Thanks.

ELAINE: So tell me, why is there a sudden silence every time I appear?

LYNN: Oh … is there?

ELAINE: *[disappointed]* Lynn.

▷ **1** *rendition:* Wiedergabe **8** *taped:* auf Band **9** *pace:* speed **11** *beckon to sb.:* jdm. winken

LYNN: Well, I mean … you can't blame people for being upset.

ELAINE: Who's upset? Are you?

LYNN: Well, no … I mean … three-and-a-half shifts are perfect for me.

ELAINE: Susan?

LYNN: Well … She really needs to save, you know.

ELAINE: Do you think some more activities would help? A party … a scavenger hunt?

LYNN: I don't know.

ELAINE: I'd really value your opinion.

LYNN: Well … if you really would …

ELAINE: Yes?

LYNN: Don't take offence … but scavenger hunts are kinda childish. I mean … Joe and Maria aren't exactly – like in grade one.

ELAINE: Joe and Maria. So, they're the ones complaining?

LYNN: No! I only used their names because they're on my team. But they have families to provide for. You realise Joe is a single parent, don't you?

ELAINE: So am I.

LYNN: You?

ELAINE: I've been providing for two daughters by myself for eleven years.

LYNN: Oh …

ELAINE: Joe's not the only person that ever got dumped, Lynn. My husband walked out after the second kid. And I didn't even have a mother to babysit for me.

LYNN: Yeah ... but you know, some people are better at coping than others.

ELAINE: Some people work at being better. I started on crew at a place like this and I worked my butt off. I went to all the social stuff, I canvassed for the charities, I did everything I was asked and a whole lot more. I got to be shift leader in six months, and second assistant manager by the end of my first year.

LYNN: Yeah, but how long were your shifts back then? I mean, Joe can't earn enough to get by ...

ELAINE: Lynn, I can't go against company policy. What good would it do anybody if I got fired?

LYNN: Yeah ... that's what my dad said ...

ELAINE: The thing is – this is my first head management job. If I show a good bottom line, they'll let me into a profit-sharing scheme. I'll be able to buy a franchise of my own. Do you know how many women get to be owners in the Kwik-Bitey's system?

LYNN: Not many I guess.

ELAINE: So, woman to woman, Lynn, I could really use a little support. Is there anything going on here I should know about?

LYNN: *[pause]* Elaine, maybe you should talk to all the guys the way you just talked to me ...

▷ **7** *scavenger hunt:* game in which people try to find objects which have been hidden **12** *take offence:* beleidigt sein **23** *dump sb.* (infml): jdn. verlassen **29** *work one's butt off* (sl): work very hard **30** *canvass for sth.:* seek support, money, etc. for sth. by going around and talking to people **33** *back then:* damals

ELAINE: You think Joe would care about my problems? It really rots his socks to have a female for a boss.

LYNN: No. He's just scared. He's afraid he's not good enough to be a father. Maybe he's not smart, but he tries. *[softer, because she sees* ELAINE *is listening]* You know, I bet … if you encourage him a little … inspire him even … I bet he'd love to be your friend.

ELAINE: *[realising she means it]* You think so? *[pause]* Perhaps you're right. *[Having made a decision, she wastes no time implementing it. To* JOE*]* Joe … in my office.

JOE *follows her off.*

SUSAN: *[lingering by the counter, as* LYNN *joins her]* What did she say?

LYNN: I feel like a sleazebag. *[to a customer]* May I take your order please?

SUSAN: Lynn?

LYNN: And will you have apple pie with that?

Sound: Repeat the 'movies out' sound cue.

LYNN: The movie's out. *[to the kitchen]* Ten straights, please.

MARIA: Where's Joe?

SUSAN: Does she suspect?

LYNN: *[to a customer]* Have a nice day. *[to another]* Welcome to our restaurant. *[to the kitchen]* Two fries, please.

MARIA *is overtaxed trying to grill and assemble and fry.*

MARIA: Susan!

LYNN: *[gesturing towards the kitchen]* Susan ...

SUSAN: Lynn, tell me what she said.

LYNN: Later. Go help Maria will you?

MARIA *screams. She's burned her hand.* LYNN *rushes to* MARIA.

SUSAN: First-aid box!

JOE: *[reappearing]* What's happening?

ELAINE: *[following* JOE *on]* Is she hurt?

MARIA: Okay. Not bad.

LYNN: It could get infected.

ELAINE: *[to the imaginary customers]* We'll be with you in a moment. *[to* MARIA*]* Let me see.

SUSAN: *[with the first-aid box]* Two lousy Band-Aids!

ELAINE: *[to* LYNN*]* She'd better go to the hospital. Go, hail a taxi. *[to* SUSAN, *as she positions* MARIA *out of the way]* Get her things from her locker. *[to* JOE*]* Take over the grill. *[to a customer, with a totally charming smile.]* I apologise for the disruption. May I take your order, please?

Sound: A montage of high-pitched activity.

▷ **1–2** *rot sb.'s socks* (infml): annoy sb. greatly **9** *implement sth.:* carry sth. out **11** *linger:* hang around, wait **13** *sleazebag* (infml): really unpleasant person **17** *sound cue:* Lautfolge zum Wiedererkennen einer bestimmten Situation **23** *overtaxed:* überfordert **33** *infected:* infiziert **36** *Band-Aid:* Hansaplast **37** *hail sth.:* call sth. (esp. a taxi) by waving in the street **39** *locker:* Schließfach **40** *disruption:* Unterbrechung **42** *high-pitched activity:* viel Aktivität

ELAINE: *[to customers]* Have a nice day. May I take your order please? And will you have fries with that? May I take your order, please? *[to* JOE*]* Great work. Keep it up.

JOE: *[with genuine admiration]* Way to go, boss.

LYNN: *[reappearing]* Come on, Maria.

Sound: Sting. The rush is over. SUSAN *appears with a bag which* ELAINE *takes from her.*

MARIA: *[protesting as* LYNN *guides her to the door]* I okay … okay.

ELAINE: It's all right. I'll pay you for the day.

As ELAINE *escorts* MARIA *off, she notices something about the feel of the bag. She peeks into it before handing it to* MARIA.

LYNN: Red crew's on.

JOE: *[coming off grill]* You seen the way the boss handled that rush?

ELAINE: *[smiling to him]* With your help. We make a great team, eh, Joe? *[to everybody]* In fact, we all make a great team.

SUSAN: Uh, oh.

ELAINE: I suppose it must seem like I forget that sometimes, but guys, listen up.

Maybe I've been inflexible
But that was yesterday
Now, there's going to be some changes
And you're all going to have your say.

I won't yell or nag or put you down
You'll find working here okay
I'll make sure you have SIX hours
and take –

JOE: Six?

ELAINE: And take home a lot more pay.

JOE: Way to go!

SUSAN: *[to* LYNN*]* You told her!

LYNN: No!

SUSAN: She's found out somehow. She must have!

ELAINE: That you're trying to cause a lot of trouble around here? Oh, yes, Susan, I've found out.

SUSAN: *[to* ELAINE*]* It wasn't just me, Elaine. Everybody voted for the union.

ELAINE: Everybody?

LYNN: Almost everybody.

SUSAN: Forty-two out of fifty-eight signed. It's too late to start being nice now.

ELAINE: Actually, I understand you're not certified yet?

SUSAN: We will be! There's nothing you can do to stop it!

ELAINE: Watch me.

Sound: Sting. ELAINE *hands* JOE *a letter.* JOE *steps forward.*

JOE: Dear Labour Board, I am writing to you of my own free will to tell you I was tricked into signing a union card.

▷ **4** *way to go* (AE sl): well done **10** *escort sb.:* go with sb. **13** *rush:* Andrang **23** *nag:* continually complain · *put sb. down* (infml): treat sb. badly **41** *certify sb./sth.:* officially recognize sb./sth. (i.e. as a union)

SUSAN: Joe!

JOE: The whole thing was started by a couple of trouble makers who promised us big wage hikes and that we'd be able to dick ... dicket ...

ELAINE: Dictate.

JOE: To dictate our own hours.

SUSAN: We never said that.

LYNN: She only said we'd have input.

JOE: *[pointing to* LYNN*]* She offered to take me out drinking if we signed.

SUSAN: That's a lie!

ELAINE:: You said you'd treat him to a celebration. Do you deny that?

LYNN: But that was after he signed.

JOE: *[pointing to* SUSAN*]* She never told us the union would take half our wages.

SUSAN: Eighteen cents an hour isn't half.

JOE: *[continuing]* Things are okay around here. We don't want a union. We don't need a union. Please don't certify one in this great place.

ELAINE: If anyone else wants to sign Joe's letter, we could put a stop to this stupid idea right now.

SUSAN: No one is going to sign a bunch of lies like that.

JOE: *[to the audience]* Just say no, okay? *[he passes out buttons]*

SUSAN: *[to everybody]* Can't you see what's happened? Elaine made Joe write that letter!

JOE: Just say no.

SUSAN: *[to everybody]* Don't sign it. Please, don't sign it!

LYNN: *[a quieter moment to* ELAINE*]* Elaine, why are you being so mean?

ELAINE: My girls aren't going to Hamburger U. They'll go to a real university, just like you. But if this union happens, I'm finished at Kwik-Bitey's. That's why I have to stop you and Susan, and stop you I will.

JOE *comes to her and proudly presents her with the letter.*

JOE: Thirteen of the guys changed their minds, boss.

ELAINE *walks to the scoreboard and changes it. YES: 29. NO: 29.*

ELAINE: You need fifty-five percent to be certified, don't you, Susan? You don't seem to have that anymore.

LYNN *and* SUSAN *turn their backs on* JOE *and* ELAINE *and all freeze.*

Sound: Bridge.

▷ **3** *wage hike:* pay rise **12** *deny sth.:* etwas abstreiten **22** *a bunch:* eine Menge **29** *mean:* nasty, unpleasant **39** *freeze:* stop moving and stand totally still

9. Counter Attack

JOE: *[coming out of freeze and producing a letter]* Hey, gang! We got a reply from the Labour Board. *[not certain of its legalese]* I think we stopped the union.

SUSAN: *[coming out of freeze]* I don't believe it!

ELAINE: *[coming out of freeze, taking the letter from* JOE, *and scanning it]* Because so many people wrote that Susan and Lynn intimidated them into signing union cards, the Labour Board refuses to certify a union in this franchise at this time.

SUSAN *grabs letter from* ELAINE *and scans it.*

LYNN: *[coming out of freeze]* But that's not fair!

SUSAN: Wait! It's not over! They want us to have a vote! A secret vote! It's going to be right here, next Saturday!

ELAINE: Joe, we start campaigning right now!

LYNN: *[to* SUSAN*]* What are we going to do?

SUSAN: Start phoning again! Look, there were twenty-nine guys who didn't sign Joe's letter ... that means they still want the union. All we need is thirty-one votes ...

LYNN: Thirty-one point nine.

SUSAN: Thirty-two then ... We just have to convince three people to switch back to our side again.

MARIA *brings on the phone to* SUSAN *and the ghettoblaster to* ELAINE. *Sound: The radio talk show.*

HOST: Our next caller is from the greater metro area ... And what's on your mind, ma'am?

CALLER: *[who might sound a lot like* ELAINE*]* Kids today! Can you believe that Susan Carter trying to form a union at Kwik-Bitey's?

HOST: What's with that girl? Doesn't she know the Soviet Union went belly up? The free ride is over, baby. If you expect your Doc Martins delivered to you on a silver platter, forget it! You know what you are, Susan. You're a KwikBrat.

JOE: Right on!

Sound: Catcalls. Cries of 'Commie scum', 'KwikBrat'. SUSAN *sinks to the floor. Everybody except* SUSAN *exits.*

▷ **2** *legalese:* language of the legal profession **6** *scan sth.:* look at sth. quickly **7** *intimidate sb.:* jdn. einschüchtern **27–28** *go belly up* (infml): collapse **28–29** *Doc Martins:* (brand name) type of shoes worn by punks, skinheads, etc. **30** *brat:* Balg **32** *catcalls:* Pfiffe und Buhrufe · *commie* (infml): communist · *scum:* Abschaum

10. Fall Out

SUSAN *punches in a number on the phone.*

SUSAN: Is Bill there, please? *[pause]* Well, would you tell him Susan Carter – *[pause]* the paper? No, I haven't had time. *[pause]* Mrs. Katzin, I'm not a communist. I just – *[a hang up, she sighs, then punches another number]* Marion, look, I wanted to talk to you about why you changed your mind ... yeah, it's Susan ... *[pause]* No, what are they saying? *[pause]* That's really dumb! I mean, what does starting a union have to do with whether I get dates or not? Anyway I've got Jerry. *[pause]* No, I couldn't go to the concert. I was working on this union stuff, which is why I'm phoning, – *[pause]* Karen Harris? *[pause]* No, no. I'm not upset. I mean, he did ask me first ... Listen, Marion, my mom's calling ... I'll see you tomorrow, okay? *[she hangs up, hesitates then punches in another number]* Jerry? Hi. *[pause]* I know, I been kinda busy ... *[pause]* Wanta go to a movie or something? *[pause]* Oh ... well, could I come over for a bit? I'm kinda down and I just need some one to talk to ... *[pause]* Oh. *[challenging]* With Karen? *[pause]* Yeah, I heard. So – see ya around I guess. *[she puts the down the phone, dejected]*

LYNN: *[entering after a pause]* Susan ... you missed that math test today.

SUSAN: Who had time to open a book?

LYNN: You're going to lose your chance for any kind of scholarship.

SUSAN: The way I'm going, I could lose my whole year.

LYNN: You ever think ... maybe ...

SUSAN: What?

LYNN: Well, is the union really worth it? I mean, if you hit the books, you could still pass, and even if you don't get a scholarship, at least you still have your job ...

SUSAN: Oh, yeah? For how long?

LYNN: It's against the law for Elaine to fire someone for trying to form a union.

SUSAN: So she fires us for having a bad attitude ... or wearing too much makeup.

LYNN: No ... she can't. Dad told her it would look vindictive if she fired you for at least six months.

SUSAN: Dad?

LYNN: Yeah.

SUSAN: Your dad is giving advice to Elaine?

LYNN: She came over to our house last night. I think she went to see a lot of parents.

SUSAN: Oh, no.

LYNN: She told dad – like how much trouble we were causing her ... how hurt she was ... and now ... it could really be a black mark on my employment record ...

▷ • *fallout:* the bad results of a situation **7** *dumb:* stupid **19** *dejected:* disappointed, depressed **35** *vindictive:* showing a desire for revenge

SUSAN: So ... what happened? Did dad say to lose the union or you lose your car?

LYNN: He didn't go ballistic. He just talked to me. He helped me to ... you know ... get things straight in my mind.

SUSAN: Let me guess ... like business is business.

LYNN: Well, it is ... and management has to do what's best for the business. I think Elaine should be allowed to pick her own team. I mean nobody is born with a right to work for her.

SUSAN: Nobody's born with a right to anything. It's like the union pamphlet says ... society ... that's government and voters and all that ... agree to make life more fair for people.

LYNN: Yeah ... but ... there's good and bad on both sides. I just think maybe it's time you sat down with Elaine and talked things over. She really wants to settle this so we won't have to vote tomorrow.

SUSAN: Why? What's she scared of?

LYNN: She's doesn't want a big deal ... more stuff in the paper or on TV.

SUSAN: She must think we're going to win.

LYNN: That's crazy.

SUSAN: Yes ... yes, she must. For heaven's sakes, Lynn, think about it ... she wouldn't be going to your father unless she was afraid people were going to vote for the union!

LYNN: But we don't need one anymore. Susan, listen ... she gave Joe and Maria extra shifts, didn't she? She's treating everybody pretty well. I mean, even you have got to admit things are better now.

SUSAN: Even me?

LYNN: Come on, Susan. You enjoy the confrontation ... like ... the attention.

SUSAN: You think I like people calling me names?

LYNN: Why else are you still fighting when there's no reason to? You do kinda get off on being a star or something.

SUSAN: I don't believe you're saying this to me.

LYNN: I'm sorry, Susan, if you won't listen to reason, I can't help you anymore.

SUSAN: I don't want your help. I don't need it either. *[LYNN exits and SUSAN calls after her.]* There's going to be a vote tomorrow, and the union's going to win!

SUSAN *exits.*

▷ **3** *go ballistic* (infml): become very angry **10** *pamphlet:* Broschüre **14** *settle sth.:* end sth. (e.g. an argument, dispute) **15** *be scared:* be frightened **29** *call sb. names:* jdm. beschimpfen **31** *get off on sth.* (infml): enjoy sth.

11. The Vote

Sound: Bridge segueing to car horns, catcalls from a circus of imaginary onlookers in the parking lot. Chants of 'Keep unions away from kids', 'Hands off our burgers', etc.

On stage ELAINE *and* JOE *are also chanting. Sound: The chant outside changes to 'KwikBrat, KwikBrat' as* SUSAN *enters.*

JOE: *[cocky]* Guess you can tell how popular you are, eh?

SUSAN: Let's just do it!

Sound: A referee's whistle. JOE *changes the scoreboard to 0 : 0.* MARIA *brings on the basketball and there's a toss up between* SUSAN *and* ELAINE. ELAINE *wins the toss and the game begins.*

MARIA *changes the score around as* ELAINE *and* SUSAN *hit or miss with their arguments.* JOE *leads the canned cheers for* ELAINE*'s side.* LYNN *leads the cheering section for* SUSAN. MARIA *is always silent.* SUSAN *and* ELAINE *could address the audience as the rest of the crew dribble and shoot.*

ELAINE: Okay. Remember, gang, you can vote yes to have a union … or no to keep the improvements I've already made.

SUSAN: If you vote no, those improvements won't last long.

The scoreboard changes. YES: 1. NO: 1.

ELAINE: The issue is all about loyalty, you understand. If you're not loyal to me, you can't expect me to be loyal to you.

SUSAN: *[blocking her]* That's a threat.

ELAINE: That's a fact. *[ducking around]* Gang, Kwik-Bitey's is holding a dinner and dance for all employees Friday night, and *[shooting]* we've got the hottest band in town!

Sound: Cheers. The scoreboard changes. YES: 1. NO: 4.

SUSAN: The money for these parties comes from the crew fund. We're paying for them ourselves! *[shooting]*

The scoreboard changes. YES: 5. NO: 4. Sound: Cheers and boos.

ELAINE: Right now, I've a few prizes to give out. For making the fry yield target ... Joe ... fifty dollars!

JOE: *[thrilled]* Yes!

The scoreboard changes. YES: 5. NO: 10.

Sound: Cheers

SUSAN: We don't need stupid competitions. We need decent wages. *[shooting]* And she shouldn't be able to make up all the rules. You shouldn't get fired for nothing! And you shouldn't have to suck up to her to get a bonus either! *[shooting]*

The scoreboard changes. YES: 11. NO: 10.

▷ **2** *chant* (n): words shouted repeatedly **6** *cocky:* frech **9** *toss up* (n): act of throwing a coin to decide who starts a game **32** *thrilled:* very excited **35** *decent:* good **37** *suck up to sb.* (infml): sich bei jdm. einschleimen

ELAINE: I reward the people who deliver! So, gang ... tell me what do we sell here?

JOE: S.O.S.

SUSAN: Save our souls.

ELAINE: And because we have the speediest service of any franchise around, we have a brand new free T-shirt for everybody.

The scoreboard changes. YES: 11. NO: 28.

Sound: Cheers.

SUSAN: *[running with the ball]* We don't need T-shirts. We need better safety conditions. We need a real first-aid box. *[missing basket]*

ELAINE: Someone forgot to fill it. That was bad. But if Susan had gone to help Maria when she called, we wouldn't have needed a first-aid box. *[shooting]*

Sound: Cheers and boos.

SUSAN: *[stopping in the middle of her run and facing the audience]* I mean, use your head, eh? *[throwing the ball away]* This isn't a game. It's all of our futures. If the union is so bad for us, why is Elaine fighting so hard? Please, guys, try to use your heads!

Sound: Cheers.

ELAINE: *[facing the audience]* That's right. Use your heads. Ask yourself why Susan is doing this? She wants to go to college, you all know that. I figure she's made a deal with the union to pave her way.

SUSAN: That's not true!

ELAINE: You want to know what is true? If you vote for the union, Kwik-Bitey's will close this franchise down. You won't get better wages. You won't get better hours. You'll all lose your jobs ... every single one of you!

The scoreboard changes. YES: 11. NO: 45.

Sound: Cheers.

ELAINE: Well, that's the end of that nonsense.

Sound: Wild cheering.

MARIA: Excuse me ...

ELAINE: Maria?

MARIA: I haven't had my turn to vote yet.

ELAINE: We wiped the floor with the union side. Your vote can't make any difference.

MARIA: I do not care. I have a right.

ELAINE: *[shrugging]* Go ahead.

MARIA *changes the scoreboard to YES: 12.*

SUSAN: *[astonished]* Maria!

MARIA: I am tired of promises. I am tired of lies. I am tired of threats. *[moving to* SUSAN*]* You are a brave woman. This way at least I say thank you.

ELAINE: Maria, you're fired.

JOE: *[a protest]* Hey, boss!

▷ **23–24** *pave sb.'s way* (derog): help sb.

SUSAN: You can't!

LYNN: Dad told you! You can't fire people for trying to unionise.

ELAINE: Her dismissal has nothing to do with the way she voted. She's been stealing the leftovers. There were three hamburgers in that bag in her locker.

Silence. MARIA *takes off her uniform and exits.*

LYNN: But Elaine ... I mean you were going to throw them out?

ELAINE: She broke the rules. Now, *[she and* JOE *turn the scoreboard round to the billboard]* I'll see you and Joe on your next shift.

SUSAN: You'll see me too, Elaine.

ELAINE: You intend to keep working here?

SUSAN: I haven't broken any rules. It's against the law to fire me.

ELAINE: Fine. You can be dining room hostess, permanently.

ELAINE *exits.* JOE *follows* ELAINE *off.*

SUSAN: *[to* LYNN*]* You didn't even vote, did you?

LYNN: I abstained.

LYNN *goes toward the counter,* SUSAN *makes a move to begin cleaning. They freeze with their backs to each other for a moment.*

Sound: Bridge crossfading to whirring of exhaust fans, sizzling beef, shake makers, bells, whistles and buzzes from other devices.

12. Going Forward

JOE *enters with an 'Employee of the Month' picture of himself, which he puts on display before taking his place at the grill.*

JOE: *[to* SUSAN*]* Some kid barfed in the men's washroom.

SUSAN *exits wordlessly.*

LYNN: *[to* JOE*]* You could have cleaned it up.

JOE: It's her job.

LYNN: She tried to start that union for you, you know.

JOE: Yeah, because she thinks I'm stupid, –

LYNN: No, –

JOE: – Just like you do. Elaine told me what you said about me. Well, I got news for you. I'm employee of the month this month. If I keep doing good, I'm going to be shift boss. Some day I'm going to own a place like this.

▷ **13** *permanently:* ständig, auf immer **16** *abstain:* not vote **19** *crossfade:* überblenden **23** *barf* (sl): be sick, vomit

ELAINE: *[entering]* Hey, gang. This attempt at unionisation has hurt our image in the community. To compensate, I'm having a car wash for charity Sunday afternoon. I expect every one of you to volunteer.

LYNN: *[a protest]* But Sunday, –

ELAINE: *[continuing over her]* And I want you to wear these new caps. *[producing one]* They only cost two dollars ... *[*JOE *groans]* I'm sorry, but there wasn't enough in the crew fund to pay for that dance band last week. *[*SUSAN *enters]* Where were you?

SUSAN: In the washroom.

ELAINE: Who gave you permisssion to go?

JOE: Hey, Elaine ...

SUSAN: I was cleaning it, Elaine.

ELAINE: Oh.

LYNN: *[to a customer]* May I take your order, please?

ELAINE: *[going to* JOE*]* Joe, I have to change your schedule. You can go home at five.

JOE: You promised me six hours!

ELAINE: Starting tomorrow you'll get two shifts.

LYNN: *[to* JOE*]* Cheeseburger, please.

ELAINE: You can have nine to noon and nine to midnight.

JOE: You're splitting my shifts?

ELAINE: No employee can work more than three hours at a time, remember?

JOE: Yeah, but Elaine …

LYNN: Joe, cheeseburger, please.

JOE: Elaine, you said … *[trying to remember]*

ELAINE: I said six hours. That's three plus three, isn't it?

JOE: My mom works in the morning.

ELAINE: Joe, Lynn gave you an order.

JOE: Yeah … *[to* LYNN*]* Thank you. *[to* ELAINE*]* What am I supposed to do with my kid, eh?

ELAINE: There's such a thing as day care.

JOE: Yeah, but there's no way I can pay for it.

ELAINE: I'm not forcing you to take the extra shift. There's a line up for jobs, you know.

JOE *slams the counter.*

One more display of temper like that and you're out of here!

LYNN: Elaine … Dad says not being fair to your employees isn't good business.

ELAINE: Lynn, there once was a man named Ray Kroc. He invented fast food. And what Ray Kroc said about business was that it is dog eat dog competition. The survival of the fittest. I keep fit. *[she turns to* JOE*]* Take off that pickle! The onion goes on first. *[back to* LYNN*]* Lynn, you have a customer, and remember, all of you, smiles are free.

LYNN: But only smiles.

▷ **7** *groan:* stöhnen **33** *day care:* Tagesstätte **38** *display of temper:* Wutanfall

JOE: *[to* SUSAN*]* What are you looking at?

SUSAN: Employee of the month.

JOE: *[thrusting the burger at* LYNN*]* Just shut up, will ya!

LYNN: *[to the customer]* Have a nice day.

SUSAN: Welcome to the KwikWorld
The World of KwikHappy

LYNN: Where the bosses are KwikCheap.

JOE: And working is KwikCrappy.

They all look at each other, and then manage to share a laugh.

JOE: I guess I've been a whopping big KwikJerk, eh?

SUSAN: Kinda, yeah.

JOE: Okay, okay … so … *[pause]* okay?

SUSAN: Okay.

LYNN: Joe, when school's over, I don't have much to do in the mornings … If you brought your daughter in here with you … I could take her to a playground, maybe.

JOE: Would you?

LYNN: Until university starts anyway.

SUSAN: Maybe I could too. At least … until … *[she breaks off]*

LYNN: Until you start college?

SUSAN: I'm looking for a permanent job for next year.

LYNN: Oh, Susan.

SUSAN: I've blown the scholarship and we all know Elaine is going to get rid of me sooner or later anyway.

LYNN: It's just not fair.

SUSAN: Lynn!

LYNN: No, really. It's not just you. She's treating everybody worse than she did before.

JOE: I guess I let her suck me in but good.

SUSAN: Hey, even I thought her improvements would last longer than one week.

LYNN: People are mad at her in a major way. [SUSAN *shrugs*] No, really. A lot of guys are saying how they wish they'd stuck with you. I sure wish I had.

SUSAN: So, why don't you do something about it?

LYNN: Me?

SUSAN: You and Joe, maybe.

LYNN: Susan, I know you got really burned, but … if we do decide to try to unionise again, you will help, won't you?

SUSAN: Yeah, I guess I'd help …

JOE: Like a lot?

SUSAN: Maybe …

▷ **8** *crappy:* very bad **10** *jerk:* idiot **29** *suck sb. in but good* (sl): totally deceive sb. **33** *stick with sb.:* stand by sb.

LYNN: Because I mean, it's got to be all of us sticking together or there's no point in trying.

SUSAN: Lynn, all of us trying to stick together is the point.

ELAINE: *[Off]* If there's time to lean, there's time to clean!

JOE: I think there's going to be a next time.

LYNN: Yeah.

SUSAN: All right!

ALL THREE: *[to the audience]* So have a nice day.

The End

1
AN INTERVIEW WITH THE AUTHOR

Anne Chislett: Hello, I'm Anne Chislett, I hope you enjoy this play. It was written because not too much is known about labour unions and why they exist in Canada. Unions, these days, are not very popular with the general public and the new world order. So the theatre and I wanted to expose kids to the possibility of action, to the history of the labor movement and to questioning the conditions that exist in the first place.

A.-R. Glaap: The first thing I was asked when telling students that *Flippin' In* is a play by Anne Chislett was: 'Could you explain to us what the name "Chislett" means?'

AC: According to one of my university professors it means 'little chisel', but I don't know. It is a very unusual name and whenever I publish something people approach me and say: 'I have that name, too. Do you know who we are?', and I say: 'I have no idea.' My ancestors came from Newfoundland a long time ago – in North American terms anyway – and brought their family history with them.

ARG: Are there any specific stages in your life which you consider have been important for your work as a playwright and artistic director. What was it really that made you become a playwright?

▷ **2** *labour union* (NAmE): trade union **12** *chisel:* Meißel **15** *Newfoundland:* the easternmost province of Canada

AC: I have loved the theatre from day one. We had a professional theatre when I was growing up, where all the kiddies were sent to Saturday afternoon. So my parents bought me a subscription and we went along. I loved it. I grew up with a love for the theatre. And in our school, which was very small, we were allowed time off to produce plays. I, of course, started writing them. I was in a Catholic school and if you wrote about the wise, the saints or the Pope, you could get time off and also you could get the stage and costumes and things. We began doing that in about grade three, a couple of girls and myself. I did most of the writing and the directing, and my friends did the acting.

ARG: Would you really call your plays 'issue plays'?

AC: I see theatre as a means of communication first and foremost and I don't think I write with any hope of changing anybody's mind hugely. But one hopes to raise a question or open a 'crack' in the mind. I think theatre, like journalism, has to catch an idea just a little before its time and ask the audience: 'Is this what you think, is that what you want?' So I do see a function for the theatre, it is not simply self-expression.

ARG: What I find remarkable about your plays is the variety of topics you deal with. Are there any particular issues that you think should be thematized in your plays?

AC: I try to shake the people who are convinced that they are right. I think the great enemy of society are people who are absolutely convinced that their point of view is the only acceptable one. So whatever I do, even when I am so committed to one view in the play, I'll try to do the absolute best I can do to present the other point of view fairly.

In terms of form and idea, the theme usually dictates the form for me. Certainly in the plays for young people the theme cannot be dealt with realistically – with four walls, with the invisible fourth wall and the three solid ones behind it. I start out with an issue or theme and then find the theatrical metaphor which most expresses that theme.

▷ **3** *subscription:* Abonnement **15** *huge:* extremely large in size or amount

ARG: Thinking in terms of, for instance, *Flippin' In*, there are a couple of valuable details in the stage directions which somehow reflect the theatricality that you have in mind.

AC: Yes, the staging, or at least some of it, is part of the message, part of the theme. For instance, the second scene: all ties in with the fast food restaurant, the way it is marketed.

ARG: What would you expect to be written on the back cover of the editions of your plays, say *Flippin' In*. My wife keeps telling me that she hardly ever reads what is written there because that would only manipulate her.

AC: I never read it either. It would certainly not be anything about me, because I don't think the writer should intrude on the play. The play has a life of its own, independent of me. I think it could be about the heroic little girl (in the play) who is a strong person, caught in an exposed position. While this play is not a tragedy, she still has a lot of elements of a tragic hero. She is forced into action because of her principles and assumes, perhaps naively, that everybody else is behaving in a principled manner and she runs into 'the world'. Yet she manages to keep her dignity.

ARG: What is the meaning of the title *Flippin' In*?

AC: 'Flipping' refers to the production of fast food. You are 'flipping the hamburger'. We tried to combine the word 'flip' with 'in' so that it means 'opting in' rather than 'going away', 'opting out'. 'Flipping in' is the opposite of 'flipping out'.

ARG: There are also characters in the play who give the audience the impression that they are flipping out.

AC: Yes, that's true. Susan leaves the franchise behind, because she cannot be there anymore. She has no future in this franchise. She is lost. But there is hope that e.g. Joe or Lynn might get it together and flip in. Susan will always be an activist. I think she will go on and become a labor lawyer or something. People in the franchise want to get rid of her. It would really be nice to have a happy ending, but that would not be the truth. I don't think theatre has the right to mislead and say: 'This will be alright,' when it really

▷ **3** *theatricality:* (here) action of recognizing that one is working with plays **5** *tie in with sth.:* fit in with sth. **12** *intrude on sth.:* interrupt sth. in an unwanted way **15** *exposed:* unprotected **18** *principled:* in an honest and moral way **21** *flip sth.:* turn sth. over quickly **23** *opt in:* start getting involved in sth. · *opt out:* refuse to be involved in sth. **24** *flip out:* go crazy; (here) avoid problems cannot be alright. You find hope, you find optimism, a reason to continue.

ARG: I think *Flippin' In* is not just about what is happening in that particular franchise. It is somehow a metaphor for activism and self-respect.

AC: Yes, for striving for anything, for taking a stand.

ARG: What about the name of this franchise, 'Kwik-Bitey'?

AC: One franchise got very austere with us. We had to be very careful, in the legal sense, so that nothing could be identified. I think McDonalds and Coca Cola are the symbols of this age, some of which may be good, some of which may not. 'Kwik-Bitey' is a composite of several fast food restaurants.

▷ **6** *take a stand:* declare your position or opinion on sth. **8** *austere:* [ɔːˈstɪr] strict; (here) causing problems **12** *composite:* made up of several different things

2
INTERVIEWS WITH TWO DIRECTORS ABOUT THEIR PRODUCTIONS OF FLIPPIN' IN

I. An Interview with Sally Han

A.-R. Glaap: What went into your production of *Flippin' In*?

Sally Han: I'll tell you how it first started. When I was working at Young People's Theatre, a large premiere theatre company in Toronto for young audiences, we were having difficulty coming up with what I thought was challenging work for teenagers. That's a very hard group of people to engage in theatre. I read a newspaper article in the business section about this kid who managed to organise a union at Harvey's, which is a fast food franchise like McDonald's, and he succeeded. Then there was another story about Sara Inglis, who failed. She was up against McDonald's, which – as we know – is a much larger corporation. To me it was fascinating that in a span of less than six months there were two young people, teenagers, part-time workers in the service industry, minimum wage-earners, who were out there trying to unionize, trying to collectively organize. I thought this was just fantastic. Anne Chislett came on board. She has a long history of social action and political consciousness plus she's a very fine writer. I was so excited. I really thought this was the very first play I know of for young audiences that addresses them as economic producers rather than consumers.

Service-industry workers are a very hard sector to organize: a) their staff turnover is incredibly high, and b) a lot of them, particularly because they are young and inexperienced, don't know that they have rights.You don't complain, they can pay you lousy, you don't know what your benefits are, fundamentally most of you aren't making a living doing this. I felt this was a play that addressed that aspect of their working lives.

I think any play which forces kids to look beyond their own world, and addresses their participation in larger social structures is good. So I thought it was really a worthwhile play to do.

▷ **15** *unionize:* organize workers into (trade) unions **23** *staff turnover:* the rate at which employees leave a company and are replaced

ARG: If you were asked to introduce students to *Flippin' In* with a couple of sentences only, what would you tell them?

SH: I would say, have you ever thought about what it means to work? Have you ever thought about what is work and what it's worth to you? What are the values of work to you other than money? In a working environment, what do you like or dislike? What is valuable to you about working? I think that opens up a whole range of questions.

ARG: How would you account for the meaning of the title *Flippin' In*?

SH: Anne and I have this endless joke about it. When I asked her what 'flippin' in' means, she said she's just really bad with titles. This is my understanding, 'flippin' out' means going crazy, so 'flippin' in' means becoming sane. The other thing, of course, with the 'flippin'' idea is that's what you do with the burgers. So instead of flippin' out the burgers to the consumer it may be, in a way, 'flippin' in' in terms of your own work, in terms of your own community, I guess. I never really knew the meaning of that title. Everytime I asked Anne, she would always give me that flip answer.

II. An Interview with Elsa Bolam

A.-R. Glaap: What made you choose *Flippin' In* for a production?

Elsa Bolam: I chose to do *Flippin' In* because I'm a mother. I have kids that are a little bit older than the kids we perform to in high school. But one is increasingly worried about the future in terms of the corporate agenda taking over the world. I think *Flippin' In* – OK, it's about unions – is very much a 'people play' and what we're asserting in doing *Flippin' In* is the value of people not being cogs in some immense machine for the benefit of these faceless corporate individuals. Unfortunately it seems almost as though the world is going in that direction. The power of advertising sort of persuades people to eat this kind of food and to think that it's cool to do so, it's a bit like cigarette advertising. People all across the world are brainwashed into thinking it's cool to have fast food.

▷ **14** *sane:* having a healthy mind **26** *corporate:* of the business world **28** *assert sth.:* state sth. very strongly **29** *a cog in the machine:* bloß ein Rädchen im Getriebe

'Have a nice day!': A scene from Elsa Bolam's production of *Flippin' In*

People in Moscow are flocking to have it thinking it's a wonderful new thing, when in fact it's rather a debasement of food. This play also deals with teenagers as an economic force and examines their points of view of why they're working in a fast food restaurant. I think Anne chose the characters very well.

ARG: Addressing you as the director, I'm interested in how you went about discussing it with actors and actresses. Did you have to read the play first? Did they come up with questions?

EB: We read it together, talked about it and read a lot of background information. We had gathered information and we made all that information available to the actors. We also used it as an opportunity to study the history of unionization in Canada. Then the actors contributed their personal experiences to it. We then got to work on the play at which point the design became predominant. We did it in a completely unrealistic way, which was a lot of fun. We did it mostly in gyms and we used the basketball net that was there for the game at the end of the game. When we played in a theatre, we took the basketball net and a pole around with us. We

▷ **1** *flock* (v): go together in large numbers **2** *debasement:* reduction in quality had our set very anonymous at the beginning, very sort of blank. At the moment when KwikWorld is mentioned we did a transformation.

ARG: How was that done?

EB: It was something very simple. It was a sign that said 'Whatever it is-High' and it transformed into a sign that said 'KwikWorld' and it had a menu on it. It was just a matter of pulling a string which allowed something to flip down. At that moment Elaine would come in in full rig wheeling in a giant hot dog. We had those absurd yellow shirts and things. And suddenly we were in KwikWorld. The members of the cast all changed their shirts and put on their baseball hats, and we went into the first rap number about advertising KwikWorld. We also brought on a giant milkshake and giant fries. We didn't have a stove, we had a giant hamburger. We assembled the hamburger bit during the rap. Somebody threw the onions and pickles over the side and we made the hamburger. We used it as the stove and produced all these small hamburgers. The hot dog we used as a counter. During the sequences where things get fast and furious, we change into this mechanical state: Will you have fries with that? Will you have fries with that? We'd whip it up to quite a frenzy when they were having to serve a huge crowd. It was a lot of fun doing it like that. We enjoyed it.

▷ **5–6** *Whatever it is-High:* Dingsbums-Schule **9** *in full rig:* in voller Montur **20** *whip sth. up:* etwas steigern, anheizen **21** *frenzy:* uncontrolled emotion or excitement

3
WHAT DO FAST-FOOD RESTAURANT WORKERS REALLY WANT?

In a test for training managers that is part of the Basic Restaurant Operations Course, trainees are questioned about their knowledge of employee's 'needs and wants'. They were asked to rank the following items in order of importance

Good working conditions
Personal loyalty to worker
Sympathetic understanding of personal problems
Promotion and growth
Good wages
Interesting work
Tactful discipline
Appreciation of good work done
Job security
Feeling in the know of things going on

Contrary to most what one might suppose, managers are told that the three most important things for workers are: first: appreciation of work done; second, feeling in the know of things going on; and third: sympathetic understanding of personal problems. Good wages are fifth on the list, promotion and growth ninth, and last on the list is good working conditions. Thus the message is made clear in the training course: only a bad manager has an unhappy crew. It is within each manager's power to provide for employee's 'needs and wants' as defined by the company.

The Many Functions of Teamwork

Identification of crew members with the restaurant and pride in the restaurant is fostered through a division between 'us' and 'them'. 'Us' includes both managers and workers, while 'them' refers to the customers. The image of 'teamwork' of all restaurant staff is

▷ **8** *promotion:* Beförderung **21** *crew:* team of people working together (in a fast food restaurant) **26** *foster sth.:* encourage sth.

promoted. Signs in the crew room exhorting the crew to more closely adhere to regulations would often end with 'Let's Keep Briarwood Number One!'
The service nature of the industry is used in the attempt to keep workers hard at work for their 'team'. Making money for Burger King is equated with treating customers properly, the responsibility of crew. A handout to cashiers to help in their training makes this explicit:

> Customer service and cultivating the good will of our customer requires the teamwork and cooperation of every person in a Burger King restaurant ... We have the best food products to serve and a pleasant, attractive place to eat. But without the personal attention to good service that only you can give, our customers may not return ... Be fast and friendly, with a 'smile'. Make the customer's visit a happy one.

Following this introduction is a declaration of service to the customer. Some excerpts are as follows:

> A customer is not dependent on us. We are dependent on him ...
> A customer is not just money in the cash register. He is a human being with feelings, like our own ...
> A customer is a person who comes to us with his needs and his wants. It is our job to fill them ...
> A customer deserves the most courteous attention we can give him. He is the life-blood of this and every business. He pays our salary.

The theory is that when customers feel and see a good attitude, they sense concern for them and their needs. This makes them like Burger King and want to return. Burger King urges employees to be pleasant, cheerful, smiling, and courteous at all times with the customers,

▷ **1** *exhort sb.:* ask sb. in a strong manner; encourage sb. **2** *adhere to sth.:* stick to sth. (e.g. rules) · *keep sth. number one:* make sure sth. remains the best · *Briarwood:* name of a franchised restaurant **6** *equate sth. with sth. else:* consider sth. to have the value of sth. else **20** *cash register:* Kasse **29** *urge sb.:* encourage sb. strongly fellow workers, and supervisors. They should also show obvious pride in their work and employment. But as Arlie Hochschild points out in *The Managed Heart*, a book about stewardesses, when spontaneous warmth becomes part of the job, workers become estranged from their own smiles. When job requirements involve appearing to love it, companies lay claim not just to their workers' physical motions, but to their *emotions* as well.

(From Ester Reiter, *Making Fast Food. From the Frying Pan into the Fryer*. McGill-Queen's University Press, Montreal & Kingston, 1996[2])

▷ **5** *estranged from sth.*: separated from sth. **6** *lay claim to sth.*: claim ownership of sth.

4
THE HISTORY OF FAST FOOD

During the last four decades, fast food has infiltrated every nook and cranny of American society. An industry that began with a handful of modest hot dog and hamburger stands in Southern California has spread to every corner of the nation, selling a broad range of foods wherever paying customers may be found. Fast food is now served not only at restaurants and drive-thrus but also at stadiums, airports, college campuses and elementary schools, on cruise ships, trains and airplaines, at Kmarts, Wal-Marts, gas stations and even hospital cafeterias. In 1970, Americans spent about $6 billion on fast food. Last year they spent more than $100 billion on fast food. Americans now spend more money on fast food than they do on higher education, personal computers, software or new cars. They spend more on fast food than on movies, books, magazines, newspapers, videos and recorded music – combined.

The rapid growth of the fast-food industry has been driven by fundamental changes in the U.S. economy. The hourly wage of the average American worker peaked in 1973 and then steadily declined until last year. Women entered the work force in record numbers, often motivated less by feminism than by a need to help pay the bills. In 1975, about a third of American mothers with young children worked outside home; today about two-thirds of such mothers are employed. As the sociologists Cameron Lynne Macdonald and Carmen Sirianni have noted, the entry of women into the nation's work force has greatly increased demand for the types of services that housewives traditionally performed: cooking, cleaning and child care. The fast-food industry has benefited from these demographic changes, supplying at low cost meals no longer prepared in the home and hiring at low wages millions of young women in need of extra income.

The McDonald's Corp. has become a powerful symbol of America's service economy, the sector now responsible for ninety percent of the country's new jobs. In 1968, McDonald's operated about 1,000 restaurants. Today it has about 23,000 restaurants

▷ **1–2** *every nook and cranny:* alle Ecken und Winkel **6** *drive-thru:* restaurant where you do not get out of your car to eat **17** *peak* (v): reach the highest point worldwide and opens roughly 2,000 new ones each year. An estimated one of every eight Americans has worked at McDonald's. The company annually trains more new workers than the US Army. McDonald's is the nation's largest purchaser of beef and potatoes. It is the second-largest producer of poultry. A whole new breed of chickens was developed to facilitate the production of McNuggets. The McDonald's Corp. is the largest owner of retail property in the world. Indeed, the company earns the majority of its profits not from selling food but from collecting rent. McDonald's spends more money on advertising and marketing than does any other brand, much of it targeted at children. A survey of American schoolchildren found that ninety-six percent could identify Ronald McDonald. The only fictional character with a higher degree of recognition was Santa Claus. The impact of McDonald's on the nation's culture, economy and diet is hard to overestimate. Its corporate symbol – the Golden Arches – is now more widely recognized than the Christian cross.

Almost twenty-five years ago, the farm activist Jim Hightower warned of 'the McDonaldization of America.' He viewed the emerging fast-food trade as a threat to independent businesses, a step toward a food economy dominated by giant corporations and a homogenizing influence on American life. Much of what he feared has come to pass. The rise of the fast-food industry has been accompanied by important changes in how America's food is produced. The centralized purchasing decisions of large restaurant chains and their need for standardized products have given a small number of corporations an unprecedented degree of power over the nation's food supply. Moreover, the success of the fast-food industry has encouraged other industries to adopt its business methods, filling America's main streets and malls with Gaps and Coconuts, Maid Brigades, Pawn Marts and Hobby-Town USAs. Franchises and chain stores have in the last twenty-five years gained a forty percent share of all retail spending in the United States. Amost every facet of American life has now been franchised. From the maternity ward at

▷ **1** *roughly:* approximately **7** *retail:* Handel **10** *brand:* Marke **21** *homogenize:* make everything the same (esp. in appearance or taste) **26** *unprecedented:* never seen or done before **30** *franchise:* business where the owner pays for the privilege of using the name of another company and receives help from the 'parent' company a Columbia/HCA hospital to an embalming room owned by the Houston-based Service Corporation International – 'the world's largest provider of death-care services', which since 1968 has grown to include 3,012 funeral homes, 365 cemetries and 156 crematoriums, and which today handles the final remains of one of every nine Americans – a person can now go from the cradle to the grave without spending a nickle at an independently owned business.

The key to a successful franchise, according to many texts on the subject, can be expressed in a single word: *uniformity*. Franchises and chain stores must reliably offer the same product or service at numerous locations. Customers are drawn to familiar brands by an instinct to avoid the unknown. A brand offers a feeling of reassurance when its products are always and everywhere the same. [...]

The McDonald's Corp. insists that its operators follow directions on food preparation, purchasing, store design and countless other minute details. When it comes to labor practices, however, the company's policy is strongly *laissez faire*. This allows operators to set wages according to local labor markets – and it absolves the McDonald's Corp. of direct responsibilty for roughly three-quarters of the company's work force. McDonald's decentralized hiring practices and the high turnover rate at its restaurants have helped thwart efforts to organize the company's workers. Whenever unions have threatened to overcome these obstacles, the McDonald's Corp. has suddenly shown tremendous interest in the well-being of these workers.

During the late 1960s and early 1970s, McDonald's organized a 'flying squad' of experienced managers who were sent to a restaurant at the moment that the company suspected union activity. The group was led by John Cooke, McDonald's head of labor relations. According to author John F. Love, 'Cooke's job was to keep the unions out.' Some employees were forced to take lie-detector tests,

▷ **1** *embalming room:* room where bodies are treated with chemicals before being buried **7** *nickel:* US coin worth 5 cents **16** *minute* [maɪ'njuːt]: very small **17** *laissez faire:* allowing a degree of freedom for others to do as they wish **17–18** *set wages:* decide the amount of money employees are paid **21** *high turnover rate:* fact that employees do not stay in a job for very long before leaving **22** *thwart sth.:* stop sth. **23** *obstacle:* Hindernis **27** *'flying squad':* team of people who rapidly move from one place to another allegedly to root out union sympathizers. Cooke confronted union organizers on 400 separate occasions and defeated them every time. Robert Beavers, a longtime McDonald's executive and board member, acknowledged that the flying squads efforts in the early 1970s prevented unions from gaining a foothold at the company.

In April of this year, workers at a McDonald's in Macedonia, Ohio, went on strike for five days. Led by Bryan Drapp and Jamal Nickens, two college students employed at the restaurant, the workers demanded better pay and protested the behavior of an assistant manager with a banner that read 'Did Somebody Say Unqualified Management?' After the leader of a Teamsters union in Cleveland expressed support for the strikers, the owner of the McDonald's agreed to most of the workers' demands. Drapp and Nickens later attempted to unionize the restaurant, without success. The two were fired in June after arriving for work with the word 'union' painted on their faces.

The federal Fair Labor Standards Act mandates that employees who work forty hours a week must be paid overtime for any additional hours. Few employees in the fast-food industry qualify for overtime – and even fewer are paid it. Rougly ninety percent of all fast-food workers are crew members. They are paid an hourly wage, scheduled to work as needed and often sent home during slow periods. Managers try hard to make sure that crew members work less than forty hours a week, thereby avoiding overtime payments. A small number of fast-food employees are paid regular salaries. At a hamburger restaurant with sixty-five workers, perhaps four or five have a contract and fixed terms of employment. They usually receive medical benefits and participate in some form of profit sharing. They have an opportunity to rise up the corporate ladder. But they also work long hours for low pay. A little-known provision of the Fair Labor Standards Act excludes 'executives' from receiving overtime. Fast-food assistant managers have for years been classified as executives, despite the fact much of their work involves preparing the food, serving customers and mopping the floors alongside their employees. According to Marc Linder, a professor at the University

▷ **1** *allegedly:* angeblich · *root sb. out:* find out about sb. so that he/she is not hired **11** *Teamster:* US truck driver **14** *unionize:* start a union **22** *schedule sb.:* organize sb.'s work time of Iowa Law School who specializes in labor-law issues, fast-food assistant managers working sixty to seventy hours a week may actually earn a lower hourly wage than some of their own crew members. A promotion may be the eventual reward for such hard work; yet most assistant managers will never receive that promotion.

A class-action suit was filed against Taco Bell in October 1996 by 800 of its former and present restaurant managers in California. The suit contended that managers were routinely forced to perform nonsupervisory tasks, to work fifty to seventy hours a week without overtime and to destroy employment records as a matter of company policy. It also alleged that Taco Bell threatened to fire managers who sought to be paid for their overtime hours and encouraged the hiring of illegal aliens to control costs. In 1997, Taco Bell agreed to pay eligible managers for any uncompensated work.

Alan B. Krueger, a professor of economics and public affairs at Princeton University, estimates that one-quarter of the workers in the restaurant industry are paid the minimum wage – a higher proportion than in any other American industry. Between 1968 and 1990, the years of the fast-food's industry's rapid expansion, the real value of the federal minimum wage declined by almost fifty percent. Despite the U.S. minimum wage's recent increase to $5.15 an hour, its real value is still twenty-seven percent lower than it was in 1968. Nevertheless, the National Restaurant Association strongly opposes any increase of the minimum wage at the federal, state or local level. The organization has joined with other business groups, such as the U.S. Chamber of Commerce, to fight against any new minimum-wage legislation in Congress. According to a survey in *Nation's Restaurant News*, an industry trade publication, the average corporate-executive salary in the restaurant industry increased by roughly nine percent last year, while the average corporate-executive bonus rose by twenty percent to reach $31,000. Restoring the federal minimum wage to its 1968 level would add less than a dime to the cost of a fast-food hamburger.

▷ **6** *class-action suit:* (hier) Klage **9** *nonsupervisory task:* work not involving the supervision of others, i.e. low grade work **14** *eligible:* having a right or entitlement to sth. · *uncompensated work:* unpaid work **29** *corporate-executive salary:* the amount of money earned by a senior manager in a corporation **30–31** *corporate-executive bonus:* sum of money received by top managers beyond their salary

(From 'Fast Food Nation' by Eric Schlosser, from *Rolling Stone*, September 3, 1998. By Straight Arrow Publishers Company, L.P. 1998.

Anne Chislett was born in 1942 in St. John's, Newfoundland. She went to university in St. John's and British Columbia, and then taught English and Theatre in high schools in Ontario. In 1980 she became a full-time playwright. She has written for stage, radio and film. Her plays have been produced throughout Canada as well as in the USA and Japan. Amongst her plays are *The Tomorrow Box* (1980) and *Quiet in the Land* (1996).

Anne Chislett was one of the co-founders of the The Blythe Summer Festival in 1975. This festival is unique in Canada as it only presents Canadian plays, especially those that have a particular relevance to the people in southwestern Ontario.

Flippin' In won the 1996 Chalmer's Canadian Play for Young Audiences Award.